POSSIBILITIES

UNREASONABLE

POSSIBILITIES

What is your
compelling story?

By Mike Jones

UNREASONABLE POSSIBILITIES
What is your compelling story?

Cover design by Phil Feller and interior design by Ted Ruybal.

ISBN-13 978-0-6154151-0-9
ISBN-10 0-6154151-0-5
LCCN 2010939821
First Edition
1 2 3 4 5 6 7 8 9 10

wisdom house
BOOKS
www.wisdomhousebooks.com

Mike Jones
Discover Leadership Training
1200 Post Oak Blvd., Suite 1711
Houston, TX 77056
713-807-9902 or 866-22WAYFO
www.WAYFO.com
info@wayfo.com

DEDICATION

This book is dedicated to all members of my team at Discover Leadership Training who have given so much to create unreasonable possibilities for themselves and others. You have inspired me with your commitment to the vision of Discover Leadership Training—thank you.

"Not Over"

TABLE OF CONTENTS

ACKNOWLEDGMENTS

I would like to thank Diana Nicholson, Barb Moses, Grechel Kelley, Karol Hartzell, and Michelle Trevino for their contribution to this book. Thanks for the many times you read my manuscript in an effort to help me produce a quality piece of art.

Special thanks to Phil Feller for designing the cover.

INTRODUCTION

The conversations we have with ourselves produce compelling stories. Every compelling story produces the reality that we experience in every given moment. Our compelling story reveals the frame of reference through which we view the events in our lives. Those frames create our assessments of everything we encounter. If the frame is negative, then the reality we create in this present moment is negative. If the frame is positive, then the reality we create is positive. Stick with me—if this is unclear, it is very likely that an unreasonable possibility is about to occur for you as you read on.

Unreasonable Possibilities focuses on helping you gain an understanding of why your reasonable frames are neither good nor bad; however, they are likely creating a reasonable, predictable future. The compelling stories you continually tell yourself have created whom you choose to be. You are today what your beliefs and thoughts have created. You are today where your beliefs and thoughts have brought you. You will become tomorrow what your beliefs and thoughts create, and you will arrive at the destination to which your beliefs and thoughts take you. I am not suggesting that there is anything wrong or broken, or that anything needs fixing, but I am saying that your reasonable, realistic, safe approach to life is not living at all—it is simply existing. It is playing not to lose; it is waiting to die.

I realize how bold that statement is. Please be aware that energy and action follow thought, and I encourage you to examine the compelling stories you are telling yourself. Be aware of your thoughts because your thoughts will become your words. Be aware of your words because your words will become your actions. Be aware of your actions because your actions will become your habits. Be aware of your habits because your habits will become your character. Be aware of your character because your character will become your destiny.

How did I personally get to the unreasonable places I have experienced in my life? My unreasonable belief in teenagers during the '80s and '90s created an opportunity for me to be honored significantly by Presidents Bush and Clinton.

I made a commitment to play full out, no matter what circumstances came up in my life. That commitment brought me the opportunity to create the unreasonable possibility of running a marathon eight months after open-heart surgery. I have experienced many of these opportunities in my life. How did I create positive outcomes that have benefitted millions of people in similarly challenging circumstances? What has been different for me, and for others who occupy this unreasonable space? What do self-actuators have in common?

How was Benjamin Franklin able to be successful? How about Michelangelo? Why was Dr. Martin Luther King so popular? What about John Fitzgerald Kennedy? They were unreasonable in their approaches to something, and they successfully produced unreasonable results. This has nothing to do with fate, talent, or luck—it has everything to do with *choice.*

That awareness certainly comes with an understanding of the domestication process—all of the things we learned from our teachers. The domestication process is a circumstance that we can view as a gift, because it provides checks and balances that allow us to determine whether you are really committed to your *Unreasonable Possibilities*. What is your compelling story?

Check out this "News Flash" on comfort zones . . .

> The Department of Health and Human Services published an article on August 24, 2010, stating that 10 million people are killed annually by stepping out of their comfort zones. Getting out of their comfort zones resulted in death for 78 percent of those who made that choice. The study further submits that the "safest individuals are those who surrender to the soul-crushing monotony of habit and then convince themselves that they have things pretty good."[1]

Okay, I am just kidding here. But can't you just hear people telling this very compelling story to themselves

---

1. "Report: 10 Million Killed Annually By Stepping out of Comfort Zones." *The Onion*. August 24, 2010. http://www.theonion.com/articles/report-10-million-killed-annually-by-stepping-out,17949/.

and to others? Many people will do almost anything to avoid change, challenging themselves, or getting out of their comfort zone.

This book inspires you to get out of your comfort zone. As the above referenced article states, you could die. Well, the truth is that every one of us will die someday; however, very few of us will ever choose to live. *Unreasonable Possibilities* will help you break through from producing reasonable, predictable outcomes to producing new powerful, positive, unreasonable possibilities in every aspect of your life. It does not matter what you have accomplished in your life—we all occupy the largest room in the house, and that is the room for improvement.

CHAPTER 1

THE TRUTH

As I began writing down all of the things I have become aware of that have benefited me on my daily journey, this book took form. The more I wrote, the more excited I became. I felt like an inventor who made a new discovery that would benefit others. I felt like a researcher who had found a cure. I felt like I had accomplished something that many said could not be done. I felt like a vessel through which an incredible truth was being funneled toward all who would choose to listen.

When I was a young boy, I began having unreasonable, weird thoughts that did not line up with what I was hearing from others. I remember wondering, "Am I from another planet? Is this my real family?" My resolve was to remain silent, and I did not begin speaking my thoughts and questioning things until I was about thirteen years old. When I started speaking and questioning, I frightened a few people. My questions and thoughts were unreasonable to them. I received guidance and reinforcement about life and an understanding of truth and beliefs from the perspectives of my mom, grandmother, grandfather, aunts, and uncles. Extended family—by way of neighbors and members of St. John Missionary Baptist Church—provided even more reinforcement of the truths and beliefs being taught to me by my family.

I heard all of these people talking and teaching—offering directions and suggestions regarding how to react to things, how I should feel about things, and what my place was. Because I did not respond to my teachers as a normal little boy would, they concluded that I was weird and unreasonable. Whenever we as human beings don't understand something, we give it an identity so that it will make sense to us.

The people in my life concluded I must be a preacher, a young man called by God to deliver the word to his people. When I asked what that meant, I was told that a preacher called by God was a peculiar person. Clearly not understanding this, I asked, "What do you mean by peculiar?" They responded that because I hung out with adults all the time, and because I was an "old soul" who said such profound and insightful things, I must be a preacher. I was given that identity because they didn't understand me.

To understand something, we must first place an identity on it. That identity frames this thing and gives it meaning to us. We all have a multitude of identities, and the identities that we accept as true determine our place in society, in our relationships, and at work.

A few months ago, I had a discussion with a few people about how identities direct our behaviors, determine our place in every environment, and regulate how we see ourselves. One of the participants in this conversation said she had attended a birthday party for a popular musical artist. When she arrived, everyone was given a name tag that identified him or her as a Guest, VIP Guest, or Elite VIP Guest. It was quite predictable how each of these groups behaved in this environment. I am still laughing out loud about her story.

When I was a young boy, I clearly bought the identity

that was being sold to me and I began studying my bible. I became a preacher. I had the opportunity to speak before the congregation, but they did not like what I had to say. My message was that nothing is wrong, nothing is broken, and nothing needs fixing. I preached that if we spent our time and energy focused on what has happened, then we reproduce more of the past. I said out loud, "You can't depend on the pastor; you need to get off the sidelines and make life happen *because of you* and not allow life to happen *to you.*" I said to them, "Stop taking your pity party to God, telling him how big your problems are. Go tell your problems how big your God is." Oops. I was not given too many more opportunities to speak after that.

I looked at the conditions of these folks to whom I was preaching, and I heard their compelling stories. I listened to their stories, and I did not understand how they were serving the same God I was. I read, "Ask and it *will* be given." I heard many of them teach, "Seek and you will find." I was taught, "Knock and the door will be opened." These were not euphemisms or concepts to me.

"I am not a victim," I often said to myself. I believed that I would become what I predominately thought about, and at the tender age of sixteen, I began breaking through the reasonable stories I was being told. I began shedding all of the identities I had been given.

This isn't a book about religion or a spinoff of the best-selling book *The Secret*; however, after having friends who have read many of these books—and more specifically, books written by Dr. Wayne Dwyer—say to me, "You could have written those books," I began reading Dr. Dwyer's books and the books of like-minded authors. Shortly after discovering these authors, I stopped looking for the return of the spaceship that had clearly deposited me on the wrong planet.

If I told you the truth, would you listen, or would you simply defend what you already believe? Why do I ask such a question? Because for so long, you have chosen to be logical, reasonable, and safe. You have been given certain identities, such as "not a morning person" and "shy." You have been told you cannot accomplish certain things because you are too short, too fat, not pretty enough, or don't have the proper resources. You have been told you are not smart enough; you don't have what it takes. You have also been told you are not in control of your reality, the time is not right, you are not ready, you will fail, and no one wants to be with you. The only reason any of it has come true is this: you believed it. You believed it, and it happened. The identities that others give you are not the truth until you accept them as truth.

Another lie you hold as truth is that seeing is believing. Therefore, you continue waiting for "someday," when you "see it," before you believe that everything you want and need is available to you. It would be unreasonable to believe that everything you want and need is available right now.

Okay, I slipped one of those profound truths in on you. How did it make you feel when you read that? *Everything you want and need is available to you right now.* You do not need more money to get it. You do not need more education, more contacts, or a better economy. You do not need more willpower. You do not need to be luckier or more attractive. In this present moment, you have everything you need: *choice*. I know that sounds like an oversimplification, but it isn't. It really is that simple, but it isn't easy. It is tough.

Did you recognize the conversation that was summoned in your head when you read those words? Did you hear the compelling story you immediately began telling yourself? Everything you have ever produced, created, or experienced is the result of the conversations you are having with yourself.

Stick with me for a moment . . . here comes more truth. It does not matter what is going on in your life in this present moment—there is nothing wrong, nothing is broken, and nothing needs to be fixed. Everything that has occurred up until now has been a conspiracy focused on your ultimate success. Do you believe that? Or are you defending the truth you have been told? If you don't know the answer to that question, check the conversation you are having with yourself.

Oh yes, you are having a conversation about what I just said. Listen closely to your compelling story. You may be in for the fight of your life as you create the compelling story to get what you want. Those lies will fight hard to survive, and they have a great support system, such as like-minded people who surround you.

It is time to take complete control of your life, and the way to do so is to understand how to take control of the conversation you are having with yourself. Everything you want and need is just a thought away. Energy and action follow thought, so look at what you are thinking.

If you want to change your life, my friends, you must change your compelling stories. The only way you will see this truth is by first believing it. Scary, I know, but it is what you have been doing all along. Now that you know, you need the courage to take personal responsibility and create what you want. You can choose whether to believe it before you see it; you are the creator of your life experiences. It is time to stop blaming God, your team at work, your mom and dad, your husband or wife, or your children.

I am offering you a warning: if you don't want any more of this truth, stop reading now. There will be no turning back beyond this point. When you finish this book, you will never be able to say you do not know the truth.

There are two choices available to you in this moment. Which one will you choose? Reasonable, existing, monotonous . . . or unreasonable, living, growing? You will make the choice toward the things to which you are most committed.

Oh, by the way. Now that you know you can choose to believe anything you want to believe, why not choose to believe in yourself?

CHAPTER 2

THE CONVERSATION

When each of us was born, people began speaking words to us. Even though we had no understanding, our teachers continued to say the same words over and over. As babies, we brought great joy to our teachers when we could repeat words back to them. Eventually, our teachers started putting meaning to the words. As we got older and began understanding the words we were being taught, we learned that these words brought meaning to life and offered us the lessons those around us deemed important for our survival. The words we were taught, when connected, formed sentences—and the sentences created paragraphs.

As I grew up, I gained the ability to understand the stories I was being told over and over. I had the tools to repeat them. Whenever I demonstrated a behavior that indicated I did not understand the story—or that I did not believe or perhaps had forgotten the story—it was told to me again. Sometimes new words accompanied a version of the story. Depending on how long it took me to understand or believe the story, the new words became louder, more passionate, harsher. They were delivered sometimes in a degrading tone. There were even times when physical chastisement accompanied these remedial lessons.

I was told stories about good and bad, dangerous and safe, attractive and unattractive, right and wrong, valuable and worthless. I was told stories about what I should do and what I should not do. I was told stories about what is acceptable and what is unacceptable, what is respectful and what is disrespectful, what is appropriate and what is inappropriate. I was told stories about sanity and insanity.

One of the compelling stories I learned was that people who talk to themselves are crazy. I believed this story, and I began telling this story to myself, over and over. It became my compelling story: a person who talks to himself or herself is crazy. I remember sitting in the back seat of my mom's car as she drove us home from church one Sunday afternoon. I saw a man standing on the street corner, waiting to cross the street. He was talking to himself, and I immediately thought, "He is crazy." It was not logical, and it was not reasonable, but it was the story I had been taught.

As I experienced life and became wiser, I began to have an awareness that the storyteller might be wrong. What I now know is that unless you realize you are talking to yourself continuously, you *will* go crazy.

We have conversations with ourselves at all times, about everything that is going on. We make an assessment of everything we experience through all five of our senses. We then create a compelling story about an experience, and our reality, truth, and belief are set in stone. It is time to check the conversation you are having with yourself. That conversation is creating everything you are experiencing in this present moment. It may be time to revise or rewrite your compelling stories.

One of the first words most of us learn is "no." Most of our early understanding is connected to what our storytellers did not want us to do. The conversations our teachers had with themselves were that teaching us what *not* to do would help us develop behaviors to keep us safe. The result is that they taught most of us how to play it safe and to be realistic, reasonable, and logical. They taught us how to avoid failure and hurt, how to avoid risk, and how to play to avoid losing.

There was not much thought given to the fact that if the first word they had taught us had been "yes," it would have produced an entirely different outcome, creating a much different energy and atmosphere in which we grew. Our teachers—parents, schoolteachers, bosses, mentors, grandparents, aunts, uncles, neighbors, sisters, brothers, church members, family friends—taught us in the very same way they were taught. They told us the compelling stories that were told to them. There was no malice; they did not know what they did not know. They never considered that we would be more open to and focused on unreasonable possibilities if we had been taught what *to* do. Believe it or not, we would have been safer.

I was teaching this lesson during a book signing at Barnes and Noble in 2000, and a person in the audience asked me a question: "So, are you saying that I should not teach my son not to run across a busy street?"

"That is exactly what I am saying," I replied to him.

"That is unrealistic," he retorted.

I said to him, "Unrealistic is an assessment made in the moment when we cannot see what someone else sees." When we see or feel that something is unrealistic, we are saying that the situation does not line up with our compelling stories. More importantly, we have just identified "unreasonable" for ourselves. We have just identified our capacity to believe.

Because some of our compelling stories are so strong, we "right fight" to defend them, even when we reach a new level of understanding and can see an unreasonable possibility created by a new story. Some of us pretend that the new story is insane because we refuse to accept something different. We are afraid of change. We are afraid to admit we are wrong, although, in essence, admitting we were wrong simply means we just learned something . . . and what is wrong with that?

My story is that if we teach children to pause, look both ways, and wait for the intersection to be clear of traffic before crossing the street, do we really need to tell them what not to do? Most of us feel that we must tell them of the consequences of crossing a busy street. We think we need to tell stories of how they could be injured or killed. We even include evidentiary data, complete with pictures of maimed or dead people who did not believe the story, as we focus on scaring our children into not crossing a busy street, thereby leaving them with limited possibilities and fear. These fears and limited beliefs ultimately rule our lives as we create little boxes to exist in as we join the crowds on the sidelines of life, waiting to die. This awareness is not intended to give you an instrument to blame others for anything that has occurred in your life, and it is not intended to make you feel guilty for what you may have created. I submit that one of the greatest gifts we have been given is choice. Again, the compelling stories you were told were the stories your teachers were told. The behaviors your teachers rewarded or disciplined you for were the behaviors for which the storytellers were rewarded or disciplined.

My suggestion is that you thank the storytellers for everything that has gone right in your life and accept personal responsibility for everything that has not. Accepting personal responsibility means the blame game ends now, which creates an opportunity to get on with your life—playing full out and living your life out loud.

It has been said that silence is golden. It is difficult to believe this when we observe how we behave today. There is so much noise. Our behaviors suggest that we hate silence. Recently, I was walking through Times Square in New York, and almost every person I passed had music in his or her ears—with the volume turned up loud—or was talking on a cell phone. I have become aware of why it is so important for most of us to live in constant noise, avoiding the silence as if it were the plague.

What I have discovered is that, lurking in the silence, waiting for an opportunity to emerge, waiting for the first chance to take control—to dictate your next reasonable, realistic, smart, logical move—is that vicarious chorus of voices from your past, repeating those compelling stories you have been told. Those compelling stories predict what you will do regarding your job, your significant relationships, your financial situation, your children, your parents, world events, the weather, gas prices, and everything else affecting you. The conversation you are having about all of these things is directly related to the compelling stories you were told. We heard these stories at home, school, church, and work, and from friends and the media. We reinforce these stories from movies, magazines, music, and the associations we choose. We surround ourselves with people who tell similar stories; we join organizations and attend functions where our stories are held as truth. The stories we choose to believe are the stories we choose to tell ourselves over and over. The stories we believe are the stories to which we are most committed. After a while, we become very good at telling these compelling stories. Before long, we have produced evidence that our story is true, and we will fight passionately to prove it.

All the words we have been taught come with definitions. The definitions give meaning to the words. The words allow us to communicate with each other in a common language. This language creates common identities we use to evaluate others and ourselves. If someone says you are tall, you have a reference to "tall" based on what you have been taught and through your experiences. If someone says you have a nice smile, you have a reference to "nice smile" based on what you have been taught and through your experiences. As you have learned and experienced life, you may have altered your reference to some of these things, based on your experiences. About 45 percent of your B.S. was in place by the time you were four years old.

Do you know what I mean when I say B.S.? Belief System . . . what were *you* thinking? About 95 percent of your B.S. was set in stone by the time you celebrated your eighteenth birthday. By the time you were eighteen, you had already repeated to yourself so many times the compelling stories you were taught that you really believed they were factual. Some of the stories sounded like this: "You are a good person." "You are beautiful." Some of the stories were, "You are lazy." "You will never amount to anything." "You will succeed at everything you do." "You are a leader." Some of the stories were, "You are smart." "You are a loser." "You are a good friend." "Nobody wants to be with you." Some of the stories were, "You have a lack of self-confidence." "You cannot trust people." "You are afraid to fail." Some of those stories were, "You are not worthy." "You are ugly." "You are not good enough."

It is very important to be aware that you can choose to believe anything you want to believe. It is equally important to believe that the stories you tell yourself over and over are the stories to which you are most committed. Perhaps you should read that again and allow it to sink in for a moment. Yes, I am clear about how much that awareness stings, but with awareness comes the opportunity to create an unreasonable possibility to reinvent yourself and get the things you want. Unfortunately, as soon as we take a step out of our comfort zone, away from our B.S., away from the land of the familiar, then that chorus of little voices—yes, you know what I am talking about, your "best friends"—step up to do the job for which they have been well trained and rewarded.

This chorus of little voices represents your past and is often conniving and scheming as it creates a feeling of guilt or of being overwhelmed. This chorus of little voices can be a charmer; it is an excellent salesperson, and it has the ability to guilt you into taking the actions you have been taught are "right." Now it is important to realize that this chorus of little voices representing your past is neither good nor bad, it just is. This chorus of little voices has come together to form one unified, powerful voice that is strengthened every time you tell one of its compelling stories.

Every second of the day, this powerful voice focuses on his survival. As soon as you step out of your comfort zone, out of the norm, out of the reasonable, out of the land of the familiar, the past begins asserting himself.

He becomes a pushy, arrogant, powerful voice that loves to take control. He is nosy, he loves to get his way, and he will remind you of everything that went wrong the last time you stepped out and took a risk. He will remind you of the last time you trusted and got hurt. He appears to be there to protect you; he assures you that he will keep you safe. He constantly reminds you of what is logical, reasonable, and realistic. You are in love with him, even though you say you are not. You say that you want to learn new things and that you are open minded; however, you continue to nurture him and affirm him, again and again.

I have said to many of my clients that if you give a dog a bone for pooping in the middle of the floor, he will continue pooping in the middle of the floor. The behaviors for which you reward yourself and others will be replicated. The time has come to go toe to toe with Mr. Past and let him know who is in control. Why is that so important? Because he is creating your future right now. You will soon learn how to create compelling stories focused on what you want, compelling stories that will produce unreasonable possibilities. Why will they be unreasonable? Because they will require you to take unreasonable actions to make them happen. You are going to learn how to talk yourself into the future you desire.

Our Belief System—B.S.—is our personal collection of compelling stories that have created the personal lens and filter through which we contextualize the way we see, hear, feel, taste, and touch the world. The stories we have learned from many different sources have some similarities, but none are exactly the same. Each storyteller shares his or her version of the story based on interpretation and understanding. We hear the stories and create our own versions of them. We believe that everyone has the exact same interpretation of the story that we created, which causes an expectation that when we tell the story, it will be understood and interpreted the exact same way by everyone. The compelling stories we believe soon become our road map to navigate all that life brings our way. In every moment, we make assessments of what is going on based on our maps. Every choice we make on our journey is viewed as either positive or negative, and our assessment is the result of our reference to our map. We assess every choice we make and every step we take as moving forward or moving backward. Prior to taking the next step on our journeys, we refer to our map to determine the choices we will make in that moment. We generally feel good about our choices because we have a compelling story that others in the Universal Human Paradigm agree with, and we have evidence to prove that the story is leading us toward the right choice. If the choice does not lead us to the desired result, we often begin blaming others or blaming the circumstances. As we enter and build relationships, we begin experiencing conflict with others who have different versions of the compelling stories we were told. When they disagree or don't understand our versions of the story, we think they must be uneducated or have no common sense. In our assessment, they just don't get it. We told them exactly what was needed, and we had an expectation they would respond in a certain way, but they did not.

They delivered something completely off our map, different from what we expected. We were disappointed or angry. Here is one example:

Some of us continue this behavior today. We are frustrated, wondering why team members at work, significant others, children, and friends just don't get it. We continue to approach these situations the exact same way over and over. Have you ever stopped to ask the question, "Who is really not getting it?" Here is a question I would like you to ask yourself: "If common sense is so common, why is it so rare?"

The conversations that we have with ourselves create interpretations, assessments, perceptions, and judgments. A compilation of all of the things we have been taught and of all our experiences has created our personal map. Our map is our reference to right or wrong, good or bad, appropriate or inappropriate, normal or weird, and logical, realistic, and reasonable. In our Leadership and Communications programs at Discover Leadership Training, we show our participants through experiential processes that it does not matter what you say; what matters is what others hear. It really does not matter what you show others; what matters is what they see. You must realize that others have been told compelling stories as well, and their stories have created their own personal maps. Your maps may be similar in some areas, but they are not the same. Here is another example that may look familiar to you:

If you expect that simply because you said what you wanted, others will deliver, then you will be disappointed, and you will generally blame others for not delivering what you expect. Your map creates your frame or reference to everything. We all have different frames and reference points, and yet most of us operate as if our frames and reference points were the same as everyone else's.

During one of the processes in our Discover U Leadership Breakthrough class, I give the participants what seems to be a very simple instruction after they have received a balloon from a staff member. The instruction is, "Blow up the balloon and take out your ink pen." Some of the balloons end up very small, others are larger, and others are so large that they are about to pop. And yes, there is that one person, sitting there with an ink pen in hand, prepared to "blow up the balloon." It is interesting to observe the facial expressions as participants look at each other, and then to hear the conversations—the compelling stories—about why their balloons look different from everyone else's balloons. They sometimes wonder aloud if anyone else in the room really heard the instructions given. It is important to be aware that your map is not the entire territory.

All of us have a map, and yes, we all have compelling stories as to why our map is right. Here is another example for you:

The stories we have been told have different reference points, which means there are variables in our perception. This is important to understand, because these different reference points are the reason for every ounce of conflict you have ever experienced. I say I love you. You say you love me. Your frame or reference to love has you treat me a certain way, and it has you expecting to be treated a certain way. My reference to love has me treat you a certain way, and has me expecting to be treated a certain way. Quite often, our frames or references are different, our compelling stories are different, and our evidence is different, which creates conflict—and the fight to be right is on! This predictable scene is playing out right now in millions of relationships, on every level. Have you ever taken the time to give up defending your truth and instead looked at the world through someone else's eyes? For many of you, that would be unreasonable, but if you have ever looked at the world through someone else's eyes, then you are clear that your map is not the whole territory; it is just *your* map.

There are different perceptions of everything. We all see things differently, based on our maps. The conversations we have with ourselves create our perceptions. When something happens, we assess it based on our own map. Someone who grew up in Canada will make a different assessment than someone from Las Vegas. A person who grew up poor will have a different assessment than someone who grew up wealthy. A person who grew up in a home with a mother and father who got along very well with each other will make a different assessment than someone who grew up in a home with parents who did not get along well at all.

Our reference to everything in the world is the result of

the compelling stories we believe and the experiences we have had. Your reference to these things may be completely different from others' references. When we find people who may have similar references, we fall in love with them because we have a lot in common. All of the different people of the world have different references to the world. We all have been taught lessons from the perspectives of our culture, race, religion, geographical location, fears, and life experiences. Our perceptions and our interpretations have no universal connection to right or wrong. Our perceptions are just our truths. Your perception may be right for you and wrong for someone else. Accept that, and move on.

We are generally connected so thoroughly to our compelling stories that it becomes our mission to prove others wrong. We tell our story over and over, working to convince others that they have it all wrong. Then come the feelings and emotions. We tell others they just don't understand us. If they did, they could see our reference to the subject, and if they could see our reference, they would surely change their minds. Some individuals feel their partners don't love or care for them if they won't argue with them. Still others feel that if you so much as raise your voice, you do not care about them. Every ounce of these feelings is controlled by the conversations we have with ourselves, and ALL of it is true to you, while ALL of it is a lie to someone else.

How many times a day do you say that something is weird or unrealistic, that someone "doesn't get it"? Have you noticed how many times you have thought, "That's not normal," or "She has no common sense." How many times have you questioned why the other person is doing something a particular way? As soon as you question something different, your boat is rocked. Something happens that is not on our map, and the alarm sounds. When something weird, strange, or unrealistic happens, some folks turn the music up loudly or get on their cell phones, focused on creating distracting noises. Many of us look for the crowd that will agree with us that something is weird.

Every time something weird or unrealistic happens, we begin telling stories to restore things to normal, to regain our balance, and to steady the boat. We are working to bring things back to a logical and reasonable state of being. When we cannot restore order, we get angry. We become bullies who work hard to make others wrong, or we assign identities that create fear. It takes courage to be in the moment with the weird and unrealistic; making the choice to do so is illogical and unreasonable, and that means you must be unrealistic. Every time something weird or unrealistic shows up, there is a lesson for you to learn—an opportunity for you to expand your map and create an unreasonable possibility. Be in the moment, and seize the moment.

One of the lessons my storytellers taught me is that it is better to give than to receive. I believed that lesson and created my own compelling stories about giving. I felt that it would be weird and unreasonable to choose myself first; however, to give anything away, I need to choose it for myself first. My storytellers said this was selfish, but one of the most powerful lessons I learned came when I became aware that I could not become a giver until I had received. This is a good time to check your own conversation.

Consider this for a moment: How can I teach others to be a powerful voice for God if I don't have a powerful voice? How will they even know what a powerful voice is unless I show them? How can I be a role model of a confident, passionate, joyful, committed, determined, enthusiastic, positive, focused man if I have not chosen those things for myself? How can I give anything away unless I possess it first? How can I demonstrate selfless-ness if I have nothing to give?

To give anything away, I must first be in possession of it. Only then is giving possible. Without the understanding of this truth, we are living an illusion, because nothing from nothing is nothing. It is time to kill that B.S.

CHAPTER 4

UNIVERSAL HUMAN PARADIGM

The Universal Human Paradigm contains established shoulds and should nots. We have socially agreed upon these norms. The Universal Human Paradigm gives us our identities, and those identities dictate our behaviors. These universal norms have established how people are to be treated, what is attractive and what is not, who is sexy and who is not, and who has more value based on financial status, ownership of things, or level of formal education. The norms tell us who the most valuable people are, based on eye color, hair color, and skin color.

Most people spend their entire lives being defined by the conversations others are having about them. The compelling stories they tell themselves about themselves are externally driven—the stories are based on their identities. People make up their faces to meet the Universal Human Paradigm's assessment of beautiful or cute. They cut or comb their hair a certain way, they wear the right clothes, they have surgery to meet the criteria of the paradigm, and for some, working out and eating certain foods has nothing to do with being healthy.

Every day, millions of people strut their stuff like a peacock on the big stage, looking for an opportunity for someone's affirming eyes to say to them, in the words of James Blunt's song, "You're Beautiful." Others are waiting for someone to affirm their handsomeness or are waiting to receive a flirtatious word or deed from another. We are so controlled by the conversations that others are having about us in the Universal Human Paradigm that we treat our children a certain way to make sure they don't display behaviors that will make us look bad. We teach them the rules. We tell them compelling stories that would have them behave in a way that will not embarrass us. These compelling stories, in turn, create their identities, and the story lives on.

How many of you remember when you were two years old, exploring your new world, learning words and sounds, learning to walk, and taking advantage of all of the new possibilities you were becoming aware of? You demonstrated your unbridled, authentic enthusiasm for this life you were discovering. And then came the storytellers, imparting upon you the gifts they received from others. I know clearly that these gifts were given in love.

The compelling stories I heard when I was two explained how I could get hurt, as my behavior was appropriate for the "terrible twos." That time period must be called the "terrible twos" because during this time, we hear two specific words used in a terrible way over and over. Those words are "don't" and "no." These words and their meanings begin definitively shaping our maps. I believe these early stories we are told, stories proceeded by "don't" and "no," teach us to play the game of life safely. They teach us to play not to lose, rather than teaching us how to play full out to win.

I call the Universal Human Paradigm "The Big Game," or "The Unaware Harmonious Population." The rules of the game are clear. Following those rules allows you to slide in under the radar, blend in with the crowd, be affirmed often, and have someone else to blame for things that go wrong.

When you play "The Big Game" with others who have been taught the same basic rules of the game regarding appearance, and these others say you look good, you feel good about yourself. When how you look does not fit the picture they have been shown and the message is that you don't look good, you feel bad about yourself. Thus, people spend a tremendous amount of time and resources hiding their perceived flaws and imperfections, turning the lights out so that others cannot see their "real" selves, hiding their little issues and problems so others will believe everything is as it should be. If those in your world could only hear your conversation behind the conversation, they would know things really are not as they appear to be.

As a result of the shoulds and should nots of "The Unaware Harmonious Population," most of us go through life "shoulding" all over each other. We focus on saying things right, wearing the right clothes, driving the right car, choosing the right career, attending the right school, and reading the right books.

When we are truly being authentic and in the moment, and when we are living in truth, focused on what we want rather than on the paradigm, we are aware that there is a difference between doing the right thing and doing things right. Doing things right usually means we are focused on what others expect from us based on who they think we are and who they think we should be. We have demonstrated consistent behaviors around others, and they now have an expectation of what doing things right means in relation to our behavior.

There was a young woman named Diana Garcia in a program I developed in the late eighties for Madison High School in Houston, Texas. This program focused on inspiring, motivating, and empowering ninth graders to accept personal responsibility for making a commitment to their educations. Diana had been given the identity of a very shy person, and she believed it. Diana believed the storyteller, and when Diana spoke, I could barely hear her voice. She was quiet and introverted. After observing Diana in the first year of this program and observing her incredible potential, I pulled her aside and told her that she would be the valedictorian of her graduating class. My gift is that I see the potential in people. Diana thought I had lost my mind; she did not have the confidence to say it, but I saw it in her eyes. Being the valedictorian meant that she would have to be outgoing, to demonstrate self-confidence, to be a leader. At that time, Diana believed she was shy, and she did not see herself as that person. That vision was unreasonable; it did not describe her.

After taking Diana and the rest of her cohorts in the peer-tutorial program through experiential processes that helped them break through their barriers and build their self-confidence, I saw them become aware of some new powerful, positive, unreasonable possibilities. These young people often delivered speeches in front of audiences large and small. We created processes through which these young people had to demonstrate the courage to ask "why?" if they did not understand something. We got rid of all the rules and asked them to enter into agreements to accomplish specific outcomes. We held them accountable for keeping their word. We taught them that their return on investment was a return on their promises. These young people became aware of the unreasonable possibilities created when they stepped outside their comfort zones and followed through with the things they committed to doing.

Diana stopped doing things right, which had affirmed that she was a shy person. She began doing the right things to drive her toward a specific, focused outcome. This was an uncomfortable time in Diana's life, but she continually pushed herself and began demonstrating unreasonable behaviors that produced unreasonable results. As a result, Miss Garcia graduated number one in her class from Madison Senior High School, and she received a full scholarship to Rice University. If Diana had done things right—done what others expected of her—she never would have achieved what she did by doing the right things.

"I will when I believe I will."

Engrave these seven words deeply in your conversation. They are packed with power. "I can" is preparing to take a step; however, it is nothing more than an acknowledgement of potential. "I will" is a verb indicating imminent action.

When we are focused on doing things right, we are generally focused on looking good for others, on meeting their expectations of us. We are concerned with what others say about us. Most people would rather lose while looking good and meeting the expectations of others than win while looking bad doing the right thing for themselves.

The right thing is determined by being focused on a specific outcome. The focused outcome allows us to know whether we are doing things right or doing the right things. When you truly understand the power that being focused on an outcome has, your motto will become iFOTO (I Focus On The Outcome).

Over 99 percent of the choices you make every day are not your own choices. Quite often, you think that because you are living, you know everything there is to know about life. You do not. Most of you will not accept that fact, but it is the truth. We all want to believe we are unique and different from others, and indeed we are in many ways. However, most of our futures are predictable because we are following the game plan of the Universal Human Paradigm.

Everything on your map—the compelling stories you are telling yourself right now—belongs to other people, and you agree with them as you continually repeat these stories. There is someone on the planet who believes the opposite of what you believe, and he or she is just as passionate about why. This is a tough awareness, so you are going to need to stick with me. Everything you learned came from another human being. Everything he or she taught you was a compelling story learned from another human being. Because of the value we gave the storyteller, we never checked to see whether the story was true.

Now we are going to do an exercise that demonstrates what we have been talking about. Please follow the instructions. In a moment, I want you to turn the page and read the information in the two boxes one time only. After you complete this process, please go to www.wayfo.com and click the "Unreasonable Possibilities" tab to record your results. I am very interested in knowing whether you get it correct the first time you read it. Remember: read it one time only.

A bird in the the hand	is worth two in the ditch!

This little exercise is an authentic way to find out a lot about yourself. First, it reveals whether you are willing to be honest with yourself. Second, it illustrates whether you are stuck in the compelling stories of your past.

Over 98 percent of the people who read the information that you just read swear that what is in the two boxes is the saying, "A bird in the hand is worth two in the ditch." When I tell them, "No, that is not what is there," they blame me for attempting to make them look bad or for tricking them. They read it again, and then they say something like this: "A bird is worth in the two . . ." I assure them there is no trick involved, that this is an authentic conversation. They get frustrated, like most of you are right now. The point is that most of you cannot see the truth in this present moment—even when it is right in front of you—because you are too attached to what somebody else said. It has been said, and most of you believe the compelling story, that seeing is believing, that the proof is in the pudding. I say that is not the truth. I have discovered that seeing is seeing. Seeing is not believing. If it is necessary for you to see it before you believe it, then you really don't believe it—you are simply agreeing with the person who showed it to you.

Yes, I am clear that the last sentence you just read isn't on your map, and it likely sounds weird and confusing.

Take a moment and read the previous page again. If you have to see it before you believe it, you are on the sidelines waiting for someone in the game to prove it to you. I am telling you that what is in those two boxes is not, "A bird in the hand is worth two in the ditch." What is there is this: "A bird in **the the** hand is worth two in the ditch." There is a double "the" there. This is how we pass on our compelling stories. Something happens, we make an assessment of what has happened based on our map, based on what we can see, based on our experiences, and we affirm the compelling story we received from someone along our journey. Then we pass the story on, never considering that we may be wrong. For everything that you can see, there is at least an equal amount that you cannot see. Every seeing has a blind spot.

If you find yourself becoming defensive every time someone points out your blind spots, you won't grow. The only benefit you will receive by totally dismissing another's offering is that you will have proved yourself right one more time. Often, we find ourselves getting defensive when someone or something pushes us out of our version of the Universal Human Paradigm, out of our comfort zone, out of our B.S., when another's compelling story is different from ours, when it is outside the land of the familiar. As we fight to hold onto our B.S., there is a battle going on inside us. Something weird happens, and it agitates the warring factions inside of us. The battle is on!

Most of us in that moment attack the thing or person outside us that stirred up this internal battle. We tell our passionate, compelling, and sometimes emotional stories—we are defending our truth, even when we know it is a lie. We continue telling these compelling stories until the behaviors supporting these stories become our habits, our outlooks on life, our beliefs of what is possible. Our fears from the past take over, and we become boring and predictable. Telling the truth would not align with what we say we believe, so we tell our compelling stories; however, the conversation behind the conversation is different—we know there is more, but it would require us to be unrealistic to claim it as ours.

If you were to put a megaphone on your compelling story, you would know that there are two stories being told: the one coming out of your mouth and the one you are having with yourself. We choose to be pretentious because the name of the game in the Universal Human

Paradigm is to look good, to sport the right identity. Your compelling story is "real," it is authentic, it is where your true feelings live. In many cases, allowing others to become aware of your compelling story would make you feel vulnerable, raw, and exposed. Telling that story may make you look bad, and people may not like or accept you. You may look and sound weird or unrealistic. So, we live our lives doing and saying things right, even when we know it is wrong.

What I really am committed to is revealed in my actions. Do not be confused by my passionate, emotional, compelling stories. My intention and my purpose resonate louder through my actions. The context of the bible verse "you will know them by their fruit" focuses on people when they are not being who they say they are.

As I let go of the past stories that hold me back, I establish a greater control of my life. I create unreasonable possibilities to move forward in a positive way. One of my life's greatest lessons came when I became aware that failure is the refusal to give up what I do not need. Things like hurt, anger, resentment, control, fear . . . the list goes on. All of these things are depreciating assets; they will never bring value. What are you holding on to?

CHAPTER 5

COMMITTED ...
OR INTERESTED?

Are you committed to being authentic? Are you committed to stepping away from the past? Are you committed to communicating effectively? Are you committed to focusing on a positive outcome? Are you committed to living in the moment? Are you committed to accepting personal responsibility? Are you committed to developing meaningful, healthy relationships? Are you committed to creating compelling stories to get what you say you want? Are you committed to doing the work and to understanding that this is a process, not an event?

If your answers to the above questions are "yes," I want you to know that this is a journey worth embarking on. I also want you to know that there is a difference between being interested and being committed. There is no neutral;

47

you are always committed to something. When we are interested, we use what I call powerless words like "I'll try," "I want to," "Maybe," or "I'll think about it," or we use what I refer to as victim statements, such as "I must," or "I have to." Did you realize that the little engine that could would not have struggled so much up that hill if his compelling story were different? His compelling story was "I think I can," and he repeated it over and over.

Let's get really clear about something. "I can" is nothing more than a statement of potential. When we are committed, we step powerfully into the commitment, affirming, "I will." We accept personal responsibility for making it happen. When we are committed, we only move forward as we focus on a positive outcome. When we are interested, the first bump in the road or the first obstacle that gets in our way or the first weird thing that happens causes us to begin backing up, making excuses, and blaming individuals and circumstances. Think about how much more powerful it would have been if the little engine had said, "I know I will, I know I will!"

At Discover Leadership Training, we begin every one of our classes by making commitments to an observable, specific outcome. We take the time to make sure everyone in the class understands the outcome we are all agreeing to, the outcome on which we will focus. First, we make sure everyone agrees that when we make a commitment to someone, we are really making the commitment or promise to ourselves. We also gain agreement that a commitment means that we will do what we say we will do, when we say we will do it, allowing no reasons, alibis, or excuses to get in our way.

We begin each of our programs with a commitment because we understand that every participant shows up with his or her very own B.S. We realize everyone has a different map. We are clear that the participants make assessments and judgments of each other and of everything going on. Everyone walks in poised to determine success or failure based on his or her expectations. The participants' expectations are connected to the references they have regarding everything the training staff says and does—because it really doesn't matter what we say to people or what we show them, what matters is what they see and hear. And what they see and hear is determined by their B.S. Making commitments allows the authentic conversation behind the conversation to be revealed. In other words, before we get started, the staff and students create an agreed-upon, compelling story about how the class is going to turn out.

I remember a TV show that was on when I was a younger man. It was called *The Flip Wilson Show*. Flip Wilson was a comedian, and one of his punch lines was, "The devil made me do it." There is nothing or no one who makes us do anything; however, how we react or respond to circumstances reveals what we are most committed to.

There is a difference between being committed and being interested. In every given moment, we are making choices. Our choices connect to outcomes. We may have chosen a positive outcome focused on what we want, or we may have chosen a negative outcome focused on what we don't want. The outcome may be survival, doing "good 'nuf," or being just good enough to get through, sliding in under the radar, underpromising and overdelivering, playing not to lose. Or, the outcome may be focused on the things you really, really, really want, with the understanding that going for what you want means taking a risk. Taking a risk means you may fail.

I believe that this thing we call failure is a gift, an

opportunity to build some iFOTO muscle. I believe failure presents an opportunity to inspire and be inspired. I believe failure is an opportunity to demonstrate what it means to be committed.

Even though you may not have demonstrated the courage to say aloud to the world what you want from your career or personal relationships, there is no question that inside your compelling story, you know what you want. Quite often, that compelling story is your biggest obstacle to getting what you want, because in everything you do, everything you want, and everything that happens, your compelling story is inserted to create your ultimate outcome.

Imagine you just got a new opportunity, one you have wanted for some time. You know what you want, and you know what you need to do to be successful with this new opportunity; however, here come the compelling stories, and now you find yourself navigating a sea of "what ifs." Some of you have a compelling story that tells you that going through this process of self-doubt is necessary. I promise to prove to you it is not.

Let's get back to the point I was making. Other than you

and God, whether anyone else knows what you want does not matter—*you* know. I often hear people whom I am coaching talking about all of the stuff they don't want. As soon as I ask them what they *do* want, they respond, "I don't know." Now we both know this is B.S., and no, I am not talking about your Belief System here.

I tell them it is impossible to say they do not know what they want, and actually not know. If they did not know what they wanted, they would not know that they did not know.

To say you don't know affirms that you have dismissed the events or offerings you have experienced or someone has suggested. Many times, we will not say what we want out loud because we lack the courage and self-confidence to play full out and go for it. Some of us feel unworthy or do not feel we can trust others to support us in our efforts to get what we want.

Saying you don't know places you firmly on the sidelines. It says you are unwilling to accept 100 percent personal responsibility. As soon as you say, "I don't know," the future is predictable. Whatever you choose to focus on in every given moment is exactly what will expand for you.

The conversation you are having with yourself—yes, I mean that compelling story you are telling yourself—is creating everything you are experiencing in every given moment. You may be looking at your boss, and your external conversation may be saying "no problem" to a request she is making of you. At the same time, your compelling story (your internal conversation) is saying, "I can't possibly get this done with everything else I need to do; it's impossible." The result is that you prove yourself right—you don't get it done, and then the blame game begins. Your compelling story is the more authentic of the two conversations.

Whatever compelling story you are choosing to believe is the story to which you are committed, and that compelling story is creating your reality. If the reality you desire isn't the one you are creating, check the conversation. Wait! Did I just suggest that you have a choice regarding your compelling story? Yes, I did. Here we go!

The answer you are seeking isn't outside you. It isn't someone else's responsibility; you must accept personal responsibility for everything going on. When you accept personal responsibility, you create an unreasonable possibility of getting one step closer to the positive outcomes you really want. When you understand the critical importance of what I am saying, your entire life experience has the potential to change completely. It is this simple: the conversation you are having right now is creating your future. If you start the project focused on a positive outcome, you don't need all of the answers in that moment. If you stay focused on your positive outcome, the answers will come. Believe it and you will see it. Conversely, if you start the project focused on everything that could go wrong, you should not be surprised when it does.

I was recently hired as an executive coach for an individual leading a large team on a 10 million dollar project. As we began this project, we uncovered some immediate issues. There was poor cross-functional communication. People who helped create the old product did not agree that it was time for a new product. Others did not believe the project could be done in the time frame being promoted. My client was stressed out with all of the potential challenges, and she began telling me her compelling story.

After listening to her story, I asked her to tell me how she wanted this project to turn out. The way I asked her to communicate this to me was in a compelling story. I asked that she write it down in past tense, as if it had happened—as if the project were complete. After she wrote it down, she shared it with me. It was amazing. Her energy while reading it had transformed her original story. She said that she wanted all of the major stakeholders on the project to write compelling stories. I agreed, and she shared her story with them and asked each of them to write a compelling story regarding his or her area of responsibility.

When we came together for the project kickoff, it was a high-energy, focused, positive party. Each of the stakeholders read his or her compelling story. People attending this event—people who had worked for this company for years—said they had never participated in a project kickoff like this before. The team was working very well at that point. Relationships transformed, and the project has already redefined every project that will follow it. What this team became aware of is that, through your compelling story, you invite whatever happens. Those thoughts are like a traffic cop giving directions toward where you focus. Please don't be surprised when you get to be right.

Be aware of your thoughts, for they will become your words; choose your words, for they will become your actions; understand your actions, for they will become your habits; study your habits, for they will become your character; develop your character, for it will become your destiny. Check the conversation.

CHAPTER 6

PERSONAL RESPONSIBILITY

No one can or has ever talked you into anything. You can choose to believe anything. Every belief you have is the result of your creating a compelling story that convinces you it is true. You talk yourself into believing the things to which you are the most committed.

Yes, others plant thought seeds in our conversation when they tell us their compelling stories. Their compelling stories come from their B.S. Sometimes, those thought seeds indicate what others are saying about you. These stories come from people who love us, and sometimes they come from magazines, movies, and music—affirming the B.S. that is taught to us from the Universal Human Paradigm.

Some of us feel good about ourselves because of those thought seeds; others feel bad. The feelings we have about what is being said are connected to the conversations we are having with ourselves. The only reason the thought seed takes root, germinates, and produces fruit is that we nurture that thought seed, water it, and fertilize it—and we believe others' compelling stories. As soon as we believe the story, energy and action follow thought, and we begin proving the stories right by producing fruit that becomes evidence.

Someone else said it about you, you agreed, and now you are affirming it. The conversation may be focused on your gender, height, hair color, weight, eye color, age, skin color, nose size, religious beliefs, or nationality. No matter what it is, it is not true for you until you create a compelling story and convince yourself it is true. You are a prophet; whatever you believe is the truth—you make it so. Once you accept that level of personal responsibility, you will never blame anyone else for anything going on in your life.

Breaking through your old behavioral, habitual patterns will be tough. My coaching to you is to embrace tough . . . fall in love with tough. There will be a new powerful, positive, unreasonable possibility created every time you do. Some of you have made the effort before, and you already know how tough it is. I assure you that the best time in your life to take this on is NOW.

However, you must be committed. If you are only interested, you will continue to wait for "someday" to happen for you. Life will happen because of you if you are committed to stepping into it in a powerful way. Life will happen to you if you continue waiting for someday. Focusing on someday means you are waiting for the right opportunity, waiting for the right person, waiting for the right job, waiting for a sunny day, waiting for the right time, and waiting for the right economy. It means you are waiting for someone to give you permission, waiting for someone to pick you to get in the game, waiting for a door to open, or waiting for a window of opportunity. When you are truly committed, there will be no excuses, reasons, or alibis for why you don't have what you say you want. When you are committed, you will create a compelling story about why you deserve what you say you want, and you will go for it with no holding back. When you are committed, if what you need does not exist, you will create it. This isn't a conversation about being selfish; this is a conversation about becoming a powerful self. This is a conversation about living, not just simply existing. This is a conversation about getting in the Big Game, reinventing yourself, redefining the rules, and playing full out.

The time to stop blaming others for anything that is going on in your life is right now. The origins of what is going on in your life are not circumstances created by others or the thought seeds they have planted. The origins of your reality in this present moment are the conversations you are having with yourself about the circumstances created by others and the thought seeds they have planted.

If you continue to consult with the past—focused on survival and playing not to lose—you *will* lose, and then you will blame the circumstances or others.

When I flew helicopters for the Houston Police Department, I met an African American police officer who had been in the helicopter division for many years prior to my arrival. This officer went into the division to fulfill his dream of becoming a pilot in this prestigious division. Many years and many opportunities passed, and he was not making his dream a reality. He was allowing the compelling stories and thought seeds of others to create fear in him. That fear paralyzed him, and he remained on the sidelines. He played not to lose by remaining a police observer in the helicopter division rather than going for what he really wanted—to be a pilot. The police observer sits in the right seat of the helicopter and communicates with the police officers on the ground. When I arrived in the division, I broke down the same walls the officer saw as impossible to penetrate. I do not mind telling you that going through the interview process and being assigned to this division was one of the most unpleasant experiences of my life. It was unreasonable that an officer with as little time on the police department could be sent to this specialized division, and a few others in the division had a B.S. that I did not belong in that division. I knew what I wanted, I set an outcome, and I broke through every circumstance I encountered until I reached my outcome.

After I successfully made it into the division and was well on my way to becoming a HPD helicopter pilot, I asked this officer why he had not taken it on to make his dream a reality. He replied, "It was like having six in one hand and half a dozen in the other; it really didn't matter."

That clearly was not true, but it was the compelling story he had created for himself to make his choice right. I remember that when he retired, he had so much anger and resentment toward the people whom he blamed for taking his dream away that he did not show up for the retirement party they arranged for him.

Talk yourself into accepting personal responsibility *now* to get the things you want out of this life. When you do, you create a new powerful, positive, unreasonable possibility by creating a compelling story that focuses on the outcome you want.

How do you know if you are stuck in past compelling stories? In every given moment, you are making choices. Every one of those choices focuses backward or it focuses forward; there is no neutral. Every one of the choices you make in the present moment creates your future. This is your now. What are you focused on?

Wow, I realize how big that is, so let's look deeper. When you step into this now moment, you have two choices: tough or suffering. Everything else is an illusion.

Tough is accepting personal responsibility. Tough is creating your compelling story, focused on what you want with no attachment to what others think, say, or do. Tough is making the choice to live instead of just exist. Tough is going for what you really, really want. Tough is creating compelling stories about who you really are and affirming those stories every day.

During a coaching session, one of my clients asked, "How do I really know who I am?"

I responded, "Whoever you are is the person you have chosen to be."

He then asked, "How do I know who I want to become?"

My response to him and to you is this: "Set a powerful, positive outcome, focused on what you really want to be. Make a commitment to making it happen, remain focused on that outcome, and observe that person emerge."

Tough—I mean really tough—is moving away from people who do not believe you can become the person you want to be. It is moving away from people, no matter who they are, who do not bring life to your journey. Tough is committing to and remaining focused on surrounding yourself with people who bring positive life energy and who support the powerful, Herculean step you are taking toward the rest of your life. Embrace tough; it will create a new powerful, positive, unreasonable possibility.

If, instead, you choose to suffer, you choose to remain stuck in those past compelling stories, existing, waiting for others to make you feel good, standing on the sidelines, waiting to die. How do you know if you are choosing to suffer? How do you know if the future you are creating is your past? It is sometimes difficult for us to see because the behaviors we have continually practiced have become habits. In many cases, we have created blind spots, and we cannot see what is right in front of us.

You are living in the past if

- You have unrealized outcomes and a list of good reasons for not taking action now to manifest them.

- You blame others for your failures and shortcomings.

- You hang on to relationships that have passed their expiration date.

- Sticking with the devil you know seems more attractive than taking the risk of creating a new powerful, positive, unreasonable possibility.

- You would rather follow the crowd than stand alone.

- You believe you are too shy to speak up.

- You choose dysfunction over confrontation.

- You really believe your situation is different from everyone else's.

- Your life is a series of "if onlys" and "what ifs?"

- You are not going for what you want because of apprehension, angst, fear, or pain.

None of the above things live outside you. All of them are created by the conversations you have with yourself. I have heard a number of people tell me over the years that they were stuck doing things the way they always had because it was too hard to teach an old dog new tricks. That is another one of those compelling stories made up by those who choose suffering as a way to convince themselves they have made the right choices.

Others have said, "This is just who I am—take it or leave it." I bet those words are actually being spoken somewhere in the world right now, and the sad truth is that someone is actually believing them. This is not who you are; this is who you choose to be. This is who you are the most committed to being, no matter how much pain you are experiencing or causing others.

Even if you don't have the courage to accept this level of personal responsibility for yourself, there is at least one more good reason why you should. Every one of us is role modeling the behaviors that emanate from our compelling stories. Much like fireflies, every human being has a light. Every thought you have produces energy and action. Are the choices you are making in this present moment producing light or darkness? Are your thoughts creating win–win or win–lose relationships? It does not matter whether you are a company president or the manager; it does not matter whether you are a parent or a grandparent, or if you are childless; it does not matter whether you live in New York or on a small island in the middle of the Pacific Ocean. You matter. Your life energy connects to the whole and produces light or darkness. Your choices create either opportunities or obstacles.

Your compelling stories create roads and bridges. Those roads and bridges urge you and others to move forward in a positive way, or they create roadblocks and barriers. We are like crabs in a bucket. When one crab chooses to grow, reinvent himself or herself, abandon the past, and escape the crab-filled bucket, others in the bucket begin telling their compelling stories based on the expectations of the Universal Human Paradigm. Their stories convince themselves and others that the individual focused on getting out of the bucket has temporarily lost his or her mind, has been brainwashed, drunk the Kool-Aid, joined a cult, or become weird.

If this courageous individual successfully gets out of the bucket—his or her comfort zone, the land of familiar—if he or she begins to reinvent himself or herself, others become so concerned that they begin planning an intervention. These crabs have convinced themselves and others that they need to save this crab from himself or herself.

If you are still stuck in the past, you are unwilling to accept personal responsibility for the choices that put you in the bucket. If you continue to focus on what happened, if you continue your commitment toward focusing on the pain of the past—focusing on what you do not want—you remain stuck in the bucket, blaming others and blaming circumstances. If you continue to bring your past into your future, you will soon experience depression. Many of you already have.

Begin right now to talk yourself into what you want. Set a positive outcome *now*, focused on what you want. Commit to moving toward gain and away from pain. Create a compelling story that says, "I am worthy, I am brave, and I am self-confident." Step powerfully into the moment, believing it and celebrating it. It will be tough, but this is your *now*. Embrace tough or suffer . . . both are available to you right now. Choose one.

CHAPTER 7

LIVING IN THE MOMENT

Prior to your arrival in this present moment, it was void of noise and void of pain. It was void of any identity until you made a choice. Now that you have chosen, what was your focus prior to the choice? What was getting your attention? Did the compelling story from your past reign superior, or did you focus on what you want—the positive outcome you set? Did you check the conversation? Did you create a compelling story that clearly moves you in the direction of your outcome? Your focus, choice, and compelling story is going to move you forward or backward; there is no zone of neutrality. The only way for the direction to be forward is to set an outcome and remain focused on that outcome in every given moment. Remember iFOTO—I Focus On The Outcome.

Our lives are a compilation of moments. Every moment affects the next, either positively or negatively; again, there is no zone of neutrality. Each moment intertwines to create the ways we experience life and the ways we deal with the circumstances that stand between us and what we want. Many times, we look at the big outcomes we have set in life—our purpose for being on this planet, the things we really want, the desires of our heart, a long and loving relationship, a successful career, healthy and confident children, a harmonious world, and financial security. As we look at all that is necessary to manifest these things, we become overwhelmed.

As you move forward, it is imperative that you make the choice to change your perceptions, change your compelling stories, and change your approach. Look at every outcome you have in front of you, and focus only on what is necessary in this present moment to continue moving forward. The choices you make now create the future. As soon as you begin changing your approach, reinventing yourself, changing your compelling stories, it will feel uncomfortable, it will feel unreasonable, it will feel unnatural, and it will feel weird. Take a moment to check the conversation, and you will soon know why you are experiencing these feelings—because the enemy has shown up. Fear of "what if" has transformed the past into your enemy. Remain focused on your outcome, and step forward powerfully into the moment . . . and that same enemy will become your ally.

How do you know whether the choice you just made in that moment was the right choice? Let's take a moment to observe the process. You set an outcome of reaching a target weight in ninety days. As you step into the next moment, it is void of noise and stories. The first thing that happens in this present moment is an assessment of all of the circumstances that get our attention—the weather, people, food aromas, and our physical wellness. If we are merely interested in the outcome of reaching a target weight in ninety days, we make one assessment of these circumstances, and if we are committed to that outcome, we make completely different assessments of the exact same things.

I will make two very important points one more time:

1. You can choose to believe anything you want to believe.

2. Your reality in this present moment is not being created by the circumstances occurring around you, it is the result of the conversations you are having with yourself about those things.

Your motto must become iFOTO. As long as you are focused on the outcome, you will know whether the choices you focus on are the optimal choices to move you forward. If we are crippled by fear and we embrace the past in that moment, that too will be obvious. If the choice we make is to bring some past compelling story— one that focuses on fear or playing it safe—to our present moment, we will get more of what we have already gotten; in other words, the results will be predictable. If we focus beyond the present moment, and our choices are made focused on what we fearfully think may happen, then again we are creating the future based on the compelling stories from our past. When we do this, our focus is generally on playing not to lose. The only way to keep moving forward is to remain focused on your outcome. The things on your map are neither good nor bad; they just are. The answer you are seeking just may be on your map; the answer in that moment may come from your past. Remain focused and committed to your outcome, and you will know the appropriate choice in that moment.

CHAPTER 8

TALK YOURSELF INTO IT

Anyone you want to be, you can become. All you need to do is talk yourself into it. Whoever you are today is a result of the compelling stories you have created and repeated to yourself over and over. Because you believe the stories, they are what get your attention, and because energy and action follow thought, these stories create your reality. When anyone or anything comes along with evidence to prove one of your stories wrong, you pull out your very own evidence and, like a skilled trial lawyer, tell your compelling story with a focus on proving the other person wrong. The only way to know with certainty that your story is a good story is to connect it to what you say your outcome is. You must remain focused on the outcome (iFOTO).

Early one Sunday morning, during one of my many visits to Campbell River, British Columbia, I was walking through a restaurant, and I heard a woman say, "Oh, my God. I hate Mondays." She had talked herself into hating Mondays because someone had planted a thought seed or because of some circumstance that had occurred once on a Monday. She created a compelling story about her good reasons Mondays deserve to be hated. What I became aware of in that moment was that Sundays could not be too much fun either, because it appeared that she began talking herself into hating Mondays on Sunday. I would imagine that Tuesdays were not a lot of fun either, as she reflected on all of the evidence from Monday that once again affirmed why Mondays deserve to be hated.

We talk ourselves into every compelling story we hold as our truth. Listen to all of the negative conversations people are having with themselves. Imagine what it would be like if there were a megaphone on every compelling story.

While I was growing up, my mom planted a thought seed in me. She said that if I went outside wet after my bath, or if I played in the rain, I would catch a cold or the flu. Someone planted that thought seed in her, and she nurtured it and watered it—and it took root. She created a compelling story and passed it on to my siblings and me. We believed her, and then we created a compelling story that reproduced the same fruit. Every time I went out wet or got caught in the rain in the winter, I expected to catch a cold or the flu. As a result, as soon as I would get a little chill, my throat would feel a little scratchy, and the compelling story I would begin to create would be, "I am catching a cold." As soon as I created that conversation, I created a possibility for it to occur—and it did. My mom would say, "See? I told you not to go out wet."

This storyteller had a lot of credibility with me, and I believed the stories she told me—and during most of my adolescent years, I had a cold year round and often battled the flu. As I became wiser, I realized that the flu and colds are associated with an airborne virus. I rewrote the story, and I talked myself into the new story. The result is that today I rarely get a cold or the flu.

There are a couple of things to be aware of as you begin the steps toward talking yourself into becoming the person you say you want to be and getting the things you really, really want. There are facts, and there are interpretations. There are few facts, but there are many interpretations. Almost every one of our compelling stories is the result of our treating our interpretations or assessments of everything that we believe as if they were facts. The result is conflict within ourselves and with others.

Here is a fact: there is abundance on this planet. However, most of us see limitations and scarcity. We spend so much time fighting over the same piece of pie, instead of simply gathering the resources needed to bake another pie. I once read, "Impossible is nothing." I believe that statement, and I have created my very own compelling story about it. I believe that the creation of our conversation that tells us something is impossible is the result of our limiting B.S., which only exists in the conversations we have with ourselves. Because energy and action follow that B.S., we never get off the sidelines to make it possible.

I experience this limiting B.S. every day with my coaching clients, with adults who attend our Master Graduate Program, with young adults in our Beyond Excellence Leadership Program, and with our teens in our Cougar

Quest and Eaglet Quest classes. We say to them, "In this present moment, you can choose to believe anything you want."

Why choose to believe that what you need to take the next step is not available to you? Why choose to believe you have a lack of self-confidence? Why choose to believe you are unworthy? Why choose to believe you will fail? Why choose to believe you have no enthusiasm? Why choose to believe you are not a risk taker? Why choose to believe you have no courage? Why choose to believe you cannot make a decision? Why choose to believe you are not beautiful? Why choose to believe you are not brilliant?

Whatever you want to become, talk yourself into it. Create a compelling story, and affirm that story every day. In fact, affirm it multiple times a day. Tell yourself, "I am positive, I am worthy, I am self-confident, and I am unreasonable." Create a compelling story that affirms, "I am courageous, I am enthusiastic, I am driven, and I am focused." Choose to set a positive outcome, and remain focused on it at all times (iFOTO).

The past will step in to defend what was. The past will remind you of everything that happened in days gone by because he wants to prove his story. You must remember that what happened in the past, happened. That is why it is called the past. Get on with living. Step into the present moment powerfully, focusing on your outcome and affirming your story. Remember that the past is not good or bad; it just is. Very likely, there are things in the past that will benefit you in the present moment. Use these things to affirm a more positive compelling story.

Choose to believe anything you want . . . talk yourself into being the person you choose to be in this present moment. You can have anything you want. The conversations you have with yourself are powerful. More than good luck or bad luck, good fortune or bad fortune, these conversations determine success or failure in everything you do.

Once, on a trip, I was picked up at the airport by a car service. When the driver met me in baggage claim, she asked me how I was doing. I answered her as I often do when people ask me that question, regardless of the circumstances going on in my life: "I am incredible; how are you?"

She huffed, "Oh, Mr. Positive. Well, I am not incredible. It has been raining all day, and business has been slow.

I guess I am okay."

I replied, "Thank you."

She asked, "What do you mean, 'thank you'?"

I told her, "We are both right." I did not hear another word from her during the hour-long drive.

My compelling story was creating the possibility of a positive future. Her compelling story was producing the possibility of a negative future, and in her opinion, she was powerless to do anything about it.

If you check the conversation you are having with yourself, you will know why you are producing the results you are experiencing. Nothing outside you is creating those results. There are those who proclaim they are saying the right things, but the words coming out of your mouth may not be aligned with what you really believe. Those words may focus more on what you believe someone else wants to hear. The outcome you produce will be the result of what you believe is true. This is not about positive thinking—it is about positive *being*.

I understand that we must start somewhere, so start talking yourself into becoming the person who will create what you want. Saying words for the sake of saying words, not believing what you are saying—these actions won't produce the results you desire. Prove it to yourself: if your compelling story focuses on what you do not want, that is exactly what you will get. It won't be long before you say, "See? I told you. This stuff doesn't work."

It is time to accept personal responsibility for everything going on in your life. It is time to turn the lights on and be real. It is time to stop telling God how big your problems are; it is time to tell the problems how big your God is. Everything you want is available to you. Set a positive outcome, and begin creating a compelling story to talk yourself into it *now*. Your motto must be iFOTO.

Below are the top seven ways of talking yourself into what you want and creating a new powerful, positive, unreasonable possibility.

1. **Set a positive outcome**. Determine what you want. Choose a positive outcome, and focus on making it happen. Your motto must be iFOTO.

2. **Create a compelling story about the outcome**. Why do you want this? How will this outcome benefit you? What will you do to make it hap-

pen? Be specific. Why is this outcome important to you? Begin visualizing the outcome as if it were already realized.

3. **List all the benefits of manifesting the outcome**. How will this outcome benefit you? How will this outcome benefit others?

4. **Affirm the compelling story daily**. Get up every day and write down your compelling story for that day—write in past tense, as if it had already occurred. What will you do today to get to your outcome? Meditate for a few moments on what you will do to accept personal responsibility for getting what you want.

5. **Be personally responsible for making choices in the moment that will get you to your outcome**. Your motto should remain iFOTO. Be committed to not blaming others or circumstances.

6. **Surround yourself with people who support you and hold you accountable**. The more you surround yourself with people who will play at this level with you, the greater your chance for success.

7. **Celebrate your victories**. Set clear milestones. Every time you succeed, celebrate. The celebration should not focus on whether or not you reached the outcome; the celebration should focus on how you played the game. If you don't hit the outcome, so what? If you played full out, celebrate. Remember, our motto is iFOTO. Refocus on the outcome, change your approach, and go for it again—this time playing full out. Changing your approach and remaining focused on your outcome produces a different result. Keep moving forward until you reach your outcome.

Talking yourself into what you want creates a new powerful, positive, unreasonable possibility *now*!

CHAPTER 9

WHAT IS YOUR STORY?

The story that is told in our obituary is a compilation of the stories we lived day after day. Every day of your life you have a choice of writing your story at the beginning of the day or reading the story of what happened at the end of the day.

Now, I realize that if you choose to write your compelling story at the beginning of your day, there will be circumstances that may happen that are completely out of your control that you did not account for. Those circumstances may completely change your story for that day; however, the ending story for that day will be a modification of what you created, as you focused on a positive outcome and accepted personal responsibility for every choice you made throughout the day. When you write your compelling story at the beginning of the day, the project, or whatever you are focused on, and when you have the courage to accept personal responsibility to make life happen because of you and to write your story as if it has already occurred, you establish the context and frame that you will be operating within. When you begin with your compelling story at the beginning, you create the attitude you will choose— no matter what circumstance comes your way.

When you wait until the end of the day, you choose to allow life to happen to you, and at the end of the day you simply get to read the story you experienced.

Here are two examples of compelling stories; begin creating your own story now.

Compelling Story #1

Woke up early today and got my run in. Nine miles at the park . . . nice cool temps, and a full moon. This morning's run was tougher than usual. I had a lot on my mind; however, I pushed through it and ran strong. I am focused! I am disciplined! I have gained the mental toughness to accomplish my outcome of running the

Houston Marathon in under four hours. Countdown: sixty-two days from today.

Took a nice hot shower, wrote in my journal, and then joined Mark for a bowl of oatmeal and fresh OJ before he headed out to the office. It was nice to have a few quiet moments with him to connect. I had my presentation with the Jennings Group today—I've been preparing for this for three months, and it's the biggest project I've gone after since I started my business last year. Landing this contract will create the foundation for taking my business to the next level, and it will bring a big income increase for my family. Mark offered his support, congratulated me for having the courage to go for it, and told me, "Be confident, Honey, and play FULL out!" I am so grateful to have such a supportive husband . . . he pushes me to reach for more, and he cheers me on!

My kids were at the door, ready to go to school right at 6:55 a.m. Wow! It is so wonderful now that they are in the groove, focused and ready for school . . . early! Because we had a few extra minutes, we put on some music, and we danced and sang. Ah, it is so cool to start the day with a party—their friends think we are all a little weird, but secretly I know my kids love it, too.

My presentation was scheduled for 2 p.m. I arrived at 1:35 p.m. As I walked into the conference room, I walked tall, shoulders back and head held high. I kept telling myself, "I am confident, I am focused, and I am driven. I have the perfect solution for the Jennings Group." I also heard Mark's voice telling me to play full out. I did! I gave 100 percent in the presentation, and they loved it . . . and guess what? I landed the contract on the spot!

I arranged for the sitter to watch the girls tonight. Today was a day to celebrate . . . I put on my favorite little black dress and texted Mark to meet me at Italiano's for dinner at 6 p.m. When he arrived, I was already there with a raised glass of our favorite wine. Cheers!

Compelling Story #2

Wow, what a day! Started off early and put points on the scoreboard for me—I got up at 4:00 and headed straight to the gym. I lifted weights and did forty-five minutes of cardio. It feels so good being disciplined with my fitness and eating commitments. My energy is great, and my cholesterol and blood pressure are back in the healthy range.

While getting ready for work, I thought a lot about how to reinvigorate the morale among my team. My company laid off three people last month, and my team took it really hard. I scheduled an all-hands meeting for this morning, and my outcome was to give my team the opportunity to express their feelings and fears, to reframe them, and to instill a shot of energy so we get back our focus on delivering with excellence.

Before leaving, I helped Sharon get the kids up so we could spend a few minutes together before we all went off to work and school. The kids love getting up early, too, because they know we always throw a party (complete with dancing and music) at the Swanson house before we go out to conquer the day. I am so grateful for the relationship I have built with my son, James. He is really responding well to the positive feedback and continual pushing. He is a natural athlete who, up until now, had some challenges academically. Thank God for Sharon. She has worked diligently to help him get on track.

My meeting with the team was OVER THE TOP! It was scheduled for 9 a.m., but when I got to the office, all of my team was already in the conference room and had requested that we start at 8 a.m. When I walked in, they shared with me that they had all met the night before, and they were ready to step up their game. They had a plan of action to get us to number one in the market. They shared that they were sad to see their team members being laid off, but they were committed to the vision of Sterling Engineering, Inc., and it was time for them to move forward and focus on a positive outcome. They asked me for my support in their plan, and without any delay, I agreed. We all cheered and got to work on the plan. My team is INCREDIBLE, and I am thrilled about our imminent success!

I left work early to watch James's baseball game. I cheered like a crazy man—what's so cool is that when I do it, then all of the other parents do, too. His team won 8–6. No surprises there . . . the Grady Red Sox have been the champions in the district for the last three years in a row. I am definitely a proud dad.

Back home, I helped Allison and Sarah with their homework, and I even enjoyed some playtime with my wife . . . We laughed so hard, we could hardly breathe. I love my life—surely, I am the most blessed man in the world!

Your Life Matters

Live your life unreasonably on purpose, because your life matters. Ready or not, someday life will end. There will be no more sunrises, no more minutes, no more hours, and no more days. All of the compelling stories you have treasured, as well as the compelling stories you taught others in the past and have long since forgotten, will pass on to someone else.

Your wealth, fame, and temporal power will shrivel to irrelevance. The grudges, resentments, frustrations, and jealousies created by your stories will finally disappear. Your hopes, ambitions, plans, and to-do lists will expire.

The wins and losses gained from defending your stories—the wins and losses that once seemed so important—will fade away. It won't matter where you came from or on what side of the tracks you lived. It won't matter whether you were beautiful or brilliant. Your gender and skin color will become irrelevant.

So what *will* matter? What compelling story will they tell about you?

What will matter and what determines the story they will tell about you is not what you bought, but what you built—not what you got, but what you gave. What will matter is not your success, but your significance. What will matter is not what you learned, but what you taught.

What will matter and determine what compelling story they will tell about you is every act of integrity, compassion, courage, or sacrifice that enriched, empowered, or encouraged others to emulate your example. What will matter is not your competence, but your character. What will matter most is not how many people you knew, but how many will benefit from your unreasonable possibilities when you're gone.

What will matter most and determine what compelling story they will tell about you are not your memories, but the memories that live on in those who loved you.

Living a life of creating unreasonable possibilities does not happen by accident. It is not a matter of circumstance, fate, or luck. Living a life of creating unreasonable possibilities is a matter of choice.

Your life matters, so choose to live your life on purpose, creating unreasonable possibilities . . . because your compelling stories will live on forever.

To learn more about Discover Leadership Training,

visit us at www.wayfo.com

ABOUT THE AUTHOR

Mike Jones is the father of four very special young men: Michael, Matthew, Christian, and Jeremy. He is a commercial multi-engine instrument rated airplane pilot and a commercially rated helicopter pilot. For the past twelve years, he has been the president of Discover Leadership Training.

During Mike's unreasonable journey, he has traveled all over the country, inspiring millions of young people to live life on purpose. He has been honored by Presidents Bush and Clinton for his commitment to the youth of our country. Mike is one of the most decorated police officers in the state of Texas. He has been featured on several national TV shows and news programs, and he enjoyed having his own television and radio programs for over ten years.

Mike has authored several books and continues to do what he loves every day in the classroom—presenting the most impactive and challenging leadership programs in the world.

CPSIA information can be obtained at www.ICGtesting.com
Printed in the USA
LVOW05s0623160514

386002LV00001B/8/P